Original title:
Finding My Light

Copyright © 2024 Swan Charm
All rights reserved.

Author: Sara Säde
ISBN HARDBACK: 978-9916-89-718-8
ISBN PAPERBACK: 978-9916-89-719-5
ISBN EBOOK: 978-9916-89-720-1

Seraphic Embrace of the Heart

In the stillness, angels sing,
Whispers of grace, a gentle spring.
Heaven's light, a guiding ray,
Leading us through night and day.

In shadows deep, we seek the flame,
Hearts ignited, in love's name.
Seraphs hover, pure and bright,
Warming souls with sacred light.

With every prayer, a soft ascent,
Rise in faith, on love dependent.
Celestial touch, a sweet caress,
In His arms, we find our rest.

When trials come, and fear appears,
Know the angels dry your tears.
In their wings, we find our peace,
Love abounds, and troubles cease.

Oh, seraphs dear, lift us high,
Into the fold, where spirits fly.
With hearts entwined in sacred art,
We dwell within the seraph's heart.

The Celestial Compass

In the heavens, a guiding light,
Stars align, dispelling night.
Whispers dance on the breeze,
Holding hopes, our hearts at ease.

Paths unfold before our gaze,
Graceful steps through life's maze.
Follow joy, let spirits soar,
Find your truth and seek for more.

With every prayer, a seed we sow,
In faith's embrace, our spirits grow.
In silent moments, we discern,
A flame within us ever burns.

Turn your heart to the skies above,
Each moment a gift, a sign of love.
The compass leads through trial and tear,
To a sanctuary ever near.

Reflections of Divine Whisper

In the stillness, soft whispers flow,
Echoes of love, a gentle glow.
Mirrored souls in sacred space,
Finding peace in each embrace.

Through trials faced, we stand united,
In faith's embrace, hearts ignited.
Reflections cast by moonlit grace,
Feel the warmth, the sacred place.

In the quiet, we boldly seek,
The voice of truth that stirs the weak.
Every moment, a gift so dear,
In divine love, we draw near.

With every breath, we sing our praise,
Guided by light through darkened days.
Whispered promises, dreams take wing,
In unity, our hearts shall sing.

Flame of the Heart's Pilgrimage

A sacred journey, step by step,
Through valleys deep, our hearts adept.
The flame within, a guiding spark,
Illuminates the path in dark.

With every challenge, courage grows,
In trials faced, our spirit glows.
Hold fast to dreams, let hope ignite,
In the silence, find the light.

We wander on, through joy and pain,
Embracing sun, enduring rain.
The heart's pilgrimage, a grace-filled art,
A journey etched in love's own chart.

Together we rise, a fortress strong,
In harmony, we find our song.
For in each flame, a promise shines,
To guide our hearts through sacred lines.

Embrace of Celestial Warmth

Under the stars, we gather close,
In celestial warmth, our spirits pose.
Each moment shared, a sacred thread,
In love's embrace, all fear is shed.

With open hearts and arms spread wide,
Finding solace as we abide.
In laughter and tears, we dance as one,
With faith unyielding, battles won.

The universe hums a soothing tune,
Beneath the sun, beneath the moon.
Every heartbeat, a prayer in flight,
In the embrace of love's pure light.

Together we rise, spirits entwined,
In celestial warmth, the truth we find.
In harmony, our souls take flight,
Guided by love, shining bright.

Voyage to Sacred Brilliance

In the stillness of the night, we sail,
Guided by stars, our hearts unveil.
Each wave whispers the secrets of grace,
As we venture forth to a holy place.

With faith as our compass, we brave the deep,
Into the light where shadows cease to creep.
The winds carry prayers on their gentle breath,
A testament to life, beyond mere death.

Every horizon a promise of hope,
In divine oceans, we learn to cope.
Together we rise, hand in hand we strive,
In the sacred brilliance, we come alive.

The journey long, yet the spirit is free,
Awash in love, we find unity.
O'er the waters of time, we glide and roam,
In the heart of the sacred, we find our home.

Upon our return, the wisdom we yield,
Transformed by the voyage, our souls are healed.
With every heartbeat, the truth we embrace,
Radiating light, in this sacred space.

Through the Veil of Darkness

Beneath the shroud of a starless night,
We seek the dawn, the return of light.
In shadows we wander, yet hope is near,
For love's gentle whisper breaks darkest fear.

Through trials and tempests, steadfast we stand,
Trusting the guidance of a higher hand.
In moments of silence, His presence we find,
A sanctuary built within the mind.

Each tear that we shed is a prayer released,
A sign of our longing for comfort and peace.
Through the veil of darkness, we learn to see,
That within our struggles, we are set free.

With each breath we take, courage ignites,
Illuminating paths in the deepest nights.
A flicker of faith, like stars in the sky,
Reminds us of promises that never die.

As dawn breaks anew, we rise from the shade,
In the warmth of His love, we are unafraid.
Through darkness and light, we journey as one,
Embracing the rise of the everlasting sun.

Radiance Revealed

In the stillness, a light begins to glow,
Soft as the breath of the evening's flow.
Hearts awaken, as grace does unfold,
A story of love eternally told.

Each moment unfolds like petals of spring,
In our souls, we feel the joy that it brings.
Through trials endured, we gather our strength,
With faith unyielding, we go to great lengths.

The whispers of wisdom, a gentle caress,
Teach us to cherish the moments, no less.
In the dance of creation, we find our place,
With each step we take, we experience grace.

When the sun sets low and shadows grow long,
We turn to the light, where our hearts belong.
In the tapestry woven by divine hands,
We discover the truth of life's greater plans.

Radiance revealed, in the depths of the soul,
Illuminates paths to make the broken whole.
In unity's arms, our spirits take flight,
Together we shine as beacons of light.

Rays of the Holy Sun

In morning's grace, the light descends,
A gift of warmth, our hearts it mends.
Each beam a whisper, soft and clear,
Guiding the lost, dispelling fear.

With every dawn, the promise flows,
Illuminating where love grows.
In sacred stillness, we arise,
To seek the truth beyond the skies.

The sun extends its golden hand,
A call to those who understand.
Awake the spirit, breathe in deep,
For blessings sown, our souls will reap.

In every shadow, light shall reign,
Through trials faced, through joys, through pain.
The holy rays, a guide so pure,
In faith, our hearts shall find the cure.

Let sunlight dance upon our brow,
To follow light, we humbly vow.
Forever grateful, we will stand,
United in this holy band.

Soul's Luminescent Mission

Beneath the stars, our spirits soar,
In search of truth forevermore.
A mission bright, a soulful quest,
To find the calm, the sacred rest.

With every heartbeat, light ignites,
A path revealed in starry nights.
The purpose clear, to love and serve,
To guide the lost, to help them curve.

Each act of kindness, gentle grace,
A reflection of the holy face.
In whispered prayers, our voices blend,
To lift the low, to heal, amend.

Through trials faced, our spirits shine,
In unity, our hearts align.
A tapestry of love we weave,
In every soul, we shall believe.

The mission calls, our hearts respond,
With open arms, our spirits bond.
Through shining light, we find our way,
A luminous journey, come what may.

A Tapestry of Divine Light

In woven threads of radiant hue,
The holy stories weave anew.
Each life a note, a sacred sound,
In unity, our hearts are bound.

From every corner, light breaks forth,
A testament of heaven's worth.
In joyful colors, love displayed,
A canvas vast, all doubts allayed.

With every heartbeat, love extends,
In harmony, the spirit mends.
Together we create the art,
A masterpiece, a sacred heart.

The tapestry, a bond divine,
In every soul, the spark will shine.
Through trials faced and shadows cast,
The light within shall ever last.

In faith we trust, in love we grow,
A journey bright, together flow.
With every thread, our stories blend,
In divine light, we find our end.

Illuminating the Forgotten Path

Upon the road, where shadows creep,
A beacon shines, the promise deep.
With gentle love, the light reveals,
The path once lost, our spirit heals.

In moments quiet, truths emerge,
A sacred guide, we feel the urge.
To lift the veil, to seek, to find,
The hidden love within mankind.

Each step we take, with faith in heart,
To heal the wounds, to do our part.
With every breath, the light shall grow,
As seeds of peace, we strive to sow.

The forgotten path, no more concealed,
In unity, our fate is sealed.
Through trials faced, through love embraced,
The shining light cannot be displaced.

So onward forth, we walk as one,
To chase the light, till day is done.
Illuminating all that strays,
With every heart, we find our ways.

Radiant Blessings Awakened

In dawn's embrace, we rise anew,
With hearts aligned and hope in view.
The gentle whispers of the day,
Guide our spirits on their way.

With every breath, we seek the holy,
In love and light, our souls unholy.
As gratitude flows like rivers wide,
In unity, in grace, we abide.

Through trials faced, we find our way,
In faith we stand, come what may.
Each moment bright, a gift divine,
Awakened blessings, forever shine.

When shadows cast, and doubts arise,
We lift our gaze to endless skies.
For in the dark, a spark ignites,
Radiant blessings, pure delights.

Let kindness bloom in every heart,
In loving hands, we play our part.
With faith ablaze, we walk together,
Awakened souls, bound forever.

Reflections of the Holy

In stillness deep, we pause to seek,
The sacred truth, the divine speak.
With open hearts, we call to grace,
In quiet moments, find our place.

The mirror shines with love so pure,
In every soul, the light's the cure.
When shadows loom, let courage flow,
For in our hearts, faith's embers glow.

Each prayer we speak, a gentle thread,
We weave a tapestry instead.
Reflections cast by sacred light,
Illuminate our darkest night.

Through trials faced, we learn to see,
The bonds that tie humanity.
In every truth, the holy beckons,
A melody of love, it reckons.

So let us walk with grace in tow,
In every step, in every glow.
Together we'll reflect the holy,
With hearts entwined, we'll stand so boldly.

The Beacon of Grace

In the still of night, a beacon shines,
Guiding lost souls through tangled pines.
With every glimmer, hope ignites,
In shadows deep, it spurs our fights.

Through storms of doubt, it leads us home,
With love as the path, no need to roam.
A gentle warmth, a soothing light,
The grace we seek through every plight.

As hearts unite, we find our way,
In whispered prayers that softly say.
With every dawn, let mercy reign,
The beacon's glow shall ease our pain.

Among the lost, we stand as one,
Through trials faced, our race is run.
With faith as our guide, we rise above,
In every deed, reflect His love.

So let this light, a guiding star,
Remind us of how blessed we are.
The beacon of grace, forever near,
Filling our hearts, dispelling fear.

The Light that Transcends

A light so pure, it knows no bound,
In every heart, its grace is found.
With every beat, our spirits soar,
For in this love, we are restored.

Through valleys deep, and mountains high,
This light will lead, as stars in the sky.
In darkest hours, it brightly glows,
A guiding flame that ever flows.

With open arms, we greet the dawn,
Each moment blessed, a gift reborn.
In unity, our voices raise,
Together we sing of love and praise.

Through every trial, the light remains,
Transcending pain, dissolving chains.
For in its warmth, our fears depart,
And fill the void within each heart.

So let us walk in this divine glow,
With every step, allow it to flow.
The light that transcends, forever near,
A symphony of hope, in hearts sincere.

Emblems of Unseen Light

In shadows deep where silence dwells,
The whispered truths of heaven tells.
Each sparkling star, a guiding flame,
In darkened night, exalt His name.

With hearts uplifted, hands that pray,
We seek the light to guide our way.
In every tear, a glimpse of grace,
The unseen love we long to chase.

In humble faith, we tread the path,
Embracing joy, forsaking wrath.
The emblems shine like morning dew,
A sacred bond, our spirits renew.

Through trials fierce, our spirits climb,
In every hymn, we sense His rhyme.
For life is lit by sacred signs,
In every soul, His love entwines.

So let us walk with fearless hearts,
As unseen light within us starts.
In unity, our voices sing,
With faithful hope, our praises bring.

The Shining Vessel of Faith

Amidst the tempest, calm and bright,
A vessel shines with purest light.
Through stormy seas, it holds its sway,
A beacon bold, come guide our way.

With tender grace, the spirit swells,
In whispered prayer, the heart compels.
Each sacred word, a precious stone,
Within the soul, a love unknown.

The vessel brims with faith divine,
A radiant glow that brightly shines.
In unity, we find embrace,
The strength of love, our saving grace.

Through trials fierce, our voyage set,
In every hope, our fears offset.
With every wave, our faith will grow,
As hearts align, His love we sow.

So let us cherish this holy craft,
In storm and calm, our souls draft.
The shining vessel, pure and true,
In faith we trust, and start anew.

Embracing the Holy Radiance

In morning light, we lift our gaze,
To holy heights, in glory's blaze.
The radiance spills like golden dew,
In every heart, love's promise true.

As petals bloom in fragrant air,
We find the warmth of answered prayer.
Embracing light, we shed our fear,
In every breath, His presence near.

With arms outstretched to heavens high,
We seek the truth that will not die.
With humble hearts, we sing His praise,
In every moment, every phase.

Through valleys low and mountains steep,
The holy radiance, ours to keep.
In silence deep, we hear His voice,
In love's embrace, we make our choice.

So let us shine with holy grace,
Reflecting light in every space.
Embracing love, a sacred art,
In every soul, His light impart.

Veils of Light Ascending

With every dawn, new veils unfold,
A tapestry of light and gold.
In sacred whispers, spirits rise,
To meet the heavens, seek the skies.

Through trials faced, we climb the height,
As faith ignites in radiant light.
The veils of doubt, they gently part,
In deeper love, we find the heart.

As golden rays break through the night,
We walk the path, our souls take flight.
With joy as strong as rivers flow,
In every step, His blessings show.

In every gaze, a glimmer clear,
The veils of light, forever near.
Through every storm, we stand our ground,
In holy love, our lives abound.

So let us rise, our hearts aligned,
With veils of light, the world entwined.
In unity, we lift our plea,
A chorus sweet, in harmony.

Touching the Hem of Glory

In silence, I kneel, heart aglow,
Yearning for peace, a gentle flow.
A touch of grace, a whisper near,
In the sacred space, I conquer fear.

With hands outstretched, I seek His light,
In shadows deep, He turns to bright.
Each tear I shed, a prayer in flight,
He lifts me high on wings of might.

The hem of glory calls my name,
In fervent hope, I stake my claim.
His love bestowed, a sacred flame,
Forever held, I am not the same.

In humble trust, I tread the path,
Embracing joy, exceeding wrath.
With every step, a vision clear,
The glory grows, I see Him near.

In unity with the divine embrace,
I find my home, my resting place.
The heart of faith, a boundless sea,
In touching grace, I am set free.

In Search of Celestial Beacons

Upon the hills, my spirit roams,
In quest of light, to find my home.
Celestial beacons guide my way,
Through night's embrace, into the day.

The stars above, a whisper clear,
Remind my heart to have no fear.
With every breath, I cleave the dark,
Toward heaven's glow, I make my mark.

In valleys low, where shadows spread,
I seek the promise, where hope is bred.
Each step I take, a prayer fulfilled,
With faith ignited, my cup is spilled.

The winds that blow, they sing a hymn,
With every struggle, my heart grows dim.
Yet still I press on, with purpose strong,
In search of chords of His eternal song.

At last, I stand where light resides,
In grace's arms, my spirit glides.
A beacon found, my soul takes flight,
In search of truth, I bask in light.

Pilgrimage to the Radiant Promise

On this journey, my heart is pure,
Every step, a sacred lure.
I traverse lands, both near and far,
Guided by faith, my guiding star.

Through trials faced, I find my way,
In darkest nights, I choose to pray.
The radiant promise shines so bright,
It fills my soul with boundless light.

With open hands, I seek to share,
The love of God that fills the air.
Every soul I meet, a gentle grace,
In this pilgrimage, we find our place.

Through whispered winds and rustling leaves,
I hear the truth that nature weaves.
A tapestry of hope unfolds,
In every story that faith holds.

At journey's end, the promise waits,
With arms wide open, love embraces fates.
In unity's song, we all belong,
This radiant promise, our hearts' lifelong.

The Unseen Guide

In the silence, He calls my name,
An unseen guide, devoid of fame.
With gentle nudges, I feel His pull,
In every moment, my heart is full.

Through crowded paths and lonely streets,
His love surrounds, my spirit meets.
With every choice, He lights the way,
Turning the night into a day.

Though veiled from sight, His presence near,
In quiet moments, He calms my fear.
Each sigh I breathe, a sacred prayer,
In all my struggles, He's always there.

In trials faced, my faith unfolds,
The unseen guide, a story told.
With hands of grace and heart so wide,
I journey forth, with Him as my guide.

As dawn breaks forth, my soul awakes,
In trust divine, my spirit shakes.
Forever bound, my heart will soar,
With the unseen guide, I seek no more.

Echoes of the Morning Star

In dawn's gentle glow we rise anew,
Hearts entwined, we seek the true.
Faith whispers soft on the morning breeze,
Guiding our souls, embracing peace.

Each ray of light, a promise divine,
Illuminates paths where we align.
With every step, we sing His grace,
In the warmth of His bright embrace.

Echoes of love in the silence reside,
As nature's chorus swells and glides.
We dance to the rhythm of His call,
In unity, we rise, though we may fall.

Hope is a flower, steadily blooms,
In our hearts, His love consumes.
Together we traverse the sacred ground,
In echoes of faith, our spirits are found.

With each breath, we honor the day,
In gratitude, we find our way.
The morning star leads us with light,
In sacred harmony, pure and bright.

Navigating by Grace

Through life's tempest, we sail along,
Anchored firmly by faith's strong song.
In shadows deep, His light prevails,
Guiding our hearts through stormy gales.

With whispers soft, He calms our fear,
In every trial, His love is near.
We navigate waters, both wide and wild,
Trusting the path like a faithful child.

Each wave we ride, a lesson learned,
In every challenge, our spirit burned.
Together we journey, hand in hand,
Stronger together, we make our stand.

Through valleys low and mountains high,
With grace as our compass, we will fly.
In unity's bond, we find our place,
Navigating life's seas, filled with grace.

As stars align in the velvet night,
We map our course, hearts shining bright.
With every heartbeat, we know it's true,
Guided by love, we will break through.

Light Through the Chasm

In darkness deep, a whisper calls,
A light that breaks through shadowed stalls.
We find our way with hearts aglow,
Through the chasm, His love will flow.

Each step we take, a prayer unfolds,
In the silence, His truth beholds.
With courage born from a sacred trust,
We journey on, for we are just.

From depths of despair, we rise and soar,
Fragmented hearts in need of more.
His light, a beacon, shines so bright,
Illuminating paths in the night.

When trials darken, and hope seems lost,
In faith unwavering, we bear the cost.
With every heartbeat, His promise is near,
Guiding us gently, casting out fear.

The chasm widens, and yet we stand,
United in love, our hearts expand.
In the light of grace, we learn to see,
That even in darkness, we are free.

Illuminated by Spirit

In quiet moments, the Spirit speaks,
A flame ignites, in silence it seeks.
With open hearts, we welcome the light,
Illuminated in His holy sight.

Each breath a prayer, a sacred song,
In the depth of our being, we belong.
He whispers wisdom, a guiding force,
In every heartbeat, we stay the course.

Through trials faced, and joys embraced,
His spirit flows, in love we're graced.
Together we rise with hands held high,
In unity, we soar and fly.

Let shadows dissolve in the warmth of the day,
As truth emerges, lighting the way.
In every moment, His presence remains,
We walk in faith, release our chains.

With gratitude deep, we open our eyes,
To see His majesty in the skies.
Illuminated by Spirit, we sing,
In the dance of life, our hearts take wing.

Illuminating the Spirit's Way

In shadows cast by doubt and fear,
The spirit glows, so bright, so clear.
Through trials faced, our hearts will soar,
With faith we tread to seek for more.

The light within, a guiding star,
It whispers truths from near and far.
With every breath, we trust and rise,
United in love, we reach the skies.

Let not the world dim our pure sight,
For in our hearts, we hold the light.
In sacred silence, wisdom flows,
The spirit's path forever knows.

In every prayer, a song takes flight,
The soul ignites in sacred night.
A journey vast, yet close at hand,
As we embark on sacred land.

And as we walk, we find our grace,
In every step, a warm embrace.
Together bound, we'll sing and praise,
Illuminating spirit's ways.

Bathed in Celestial Fire

With every dawn, we rise anew,
Bathed in light, the spirit's hue.
A flame ignites within our soul,
In sacred fire, we feel made whole.

Through trials faced, our hearts grow strong,
In unity, we sing our song.
The warmth of love, a guiding blaze,
In every breath, we lift our gaze.

Lifted high on wings of grace,
The spirit's love, our sacred space.
We dance with joy, our spirits lift,
In every moment, a treasured gift.

As shadows flee before the glow,
We seek the light, our spirits grow.
The fire brightens paths unknown,
In love's embrace, we are not alone.

With gratitude, we claim our share,
Bathed in flames, we feel the care.
Together we strive, with hearts afire,
Igniting dreams of pure desire.

Dawn's Embrace of the Spirit

In quiet morn, where whispers dwell,
The dawn unfolds, a magic spell.
With arms wide open, spirits rise,
In the embrace of painted skies.

The golden rays bring hope anew,
A tapestry of vibrant hue.
With every heartbeat, blessings flow,
In nature's grace, our spirits grow.

Together as one, we walk this land,
In gentle peace, we join hand in hand.
With every step, our hearts aligned,
In dawn's embrace, true love we find.

The air is thick with sacred light,
As souls unite in pure delight.
In every breath, a promise made,
In unity, our fears allayed.

As dawn breaks forth, we feel its bliss,
In sacred moments, hearts will kiss.
Together in this dance sublime,
Awakening to love's sweet rhyme.

The Luminous Pathway

Along the path where spirits guide,
We walk in grace, with hearts open wide.
In every heartbeat, truth is found,
On luminous pathways, we are bound.

The stars above, a beacon bright,
They shine upon our quest for light.
With every step, our spirits soar,
In harmony, we seek for more.

Through valleys deep and mountains high,
We carry forth, our spirits fly.
With gratitude, we share this flame,
In every journey, honor the name.

The road unfolds with every prayer,
In every moment, love we share.
Together we tread, hand in hand,
In the luminous light of sacred land.

As twilight falls and day departs,
We gather close, united hearts.
In sacred love, we find our way,
On the luminous pathway, come what may.

Transcending Shadows

In the depths where silence dwells,
A whisper calls, a soul compels.
Through the night, where darkness roams,
We seek the light, we find our homes.

Faith emerges, sheer and bright,
Guiding hearts towards the light.
In shadows cast, we find our way,
A path of hope for each new day.

With heavy hearts, we rise again,
Through trials faced, through joy and pain.
In every tear, a lesson grows,
In every heart, a spirit glows.

Together we stand, hand in hand,
Through storms of doubt, a sacred band.
Transcend the shadows, break the chains,
In unity, our spirit reigns.

So let the echoes of love sing,
In every heart, a sacred spring.
With every breath, let courage soar,
For in our souls, we find much more.

Love's Resplendent Illusion

In the realm of dreams divine,
Love's sweet echo starts to shine.
Each whispered word, a tender grace,
In fleeting time, we find our place.

With open arms, the heart awaits,
In every glance, the soul creates.
Illusions dance, yet truth remains,
In love's embrace, no heart contains.

Moments shared like fleeting stars,
Revealing beauty, healing scars.
A radiant glow, a gentle sigh,
As love transcends the reason why.

In laughter's tune and tears that blend,
The journey's grace, the heart will mend.
Through trials faced, through shadows cast,
Love's resplendence holds us fast.

So let us cherish every spark,
In this symphony, we find our mark.
For in love's light, illusions fall,
And in that glow, we find our all.

The Light of Compassion

A beacon bright in darkest hours,
Compassion blooms like tender flowers.
In every heart where kindness grows,
The light of love forever glows.

With gentle hands, we mend the pain,
In shared embrace, the loss we gain.
As warmth flows through each fragile thread,
A tapestry, where hope is spread.

In whispers soft, we lift the veil,
Through trials faced, we still prevail.
The light of compassion pierces night,
Illuminating paths of right.

Each humble act, a sacred gift,
In troubled waters, spirits lift.
Together we stand, forever linked,
In every word, our souls are inked.

So let compassion guide our way,
In every dawn, a new display.
For in that light, our purpose shines,
In every heart, true love aligns.

Finding Solace in Luminescence

In twilight's glow, we search for peace,
Where worries fade, and grief will cease.
In every star that lights the night,
A promise whispers, all is right.

Through darkened woods, our journey leads,
In silence deep, the spirit feeds.
We wander lost, yet find our way,
In every dawn, a brand new day.

Luminescence brightens paths anew,
With every step, a clearer view.
In shadows deep, a strength emerges,
In light we trust, our hearts converges.

Through gentle whispers, truth unfolds,
A shared embrace, the warmth it holds.
In every glance, a chance to rise,
In every heart, a light that ties.

So let us gather, souls aligned,
In luminescence, peace we find.
Through darkest nights, our spirits soar,
In unity, we are much more.

Embracing the Sacred Flame

In the stillness of the night,
We gather 'round the light,
With hearts ignited by His grace,
In this holy, sacred place.

The flicker dances in our souls,
Casting warmth, making us whole,
Each candle a prayer to the sky,
Our spirits soar, and we fly high.

With hands uplifted, we receive,
The wisdom that the ancients weave,
In every whisper, a voice divine,
Embracing love, forever shine.

Through trials faced, we stand in faith,
Each moment a chance to be wraith,
In joy and sorrow, trust in the flame,
With every heartbeat, we praise His name.

Together we rise, a chorus bright,
In the depths of day, and the darkest night,
Towards the heavens, our spirits climb,
Embracing the Sacred, transcending time.

The Journey to Inner Brilliance

In silence we seek the truth we hold,
Guided by stars, ancient and bold,
Each step we tread, a prayer profound,
In the sacred stillness, grace is found.

Through valleys low and mountains steep,
In every shadow, wisdom we reap,
The heart as compass, the soul as guide,
In the journey of love, we do not hide.

Beneath the surface, brilliance gleams,
Reflecting faith in our quiet dreams,
With every breath, we uncover the light,
In the darkest moments, ignite our sight.

In unity, our spirits soar,
Embracing challenges, seeking more,
The path unfolds, painted in gold,
Each moment a story waiting to be told.

Through night's embrace and dawn's sweet grace,
We journey forth at a steady pace,
For within us all, a treasure lies,
The journey to brilliance, beneath the skies.

Celestial Echoes of Hope

In the whispers of the night,
Stars weave tales of hope and light,
Every twinkle a promise made,
In the cosmos, fears allayed.

Through cosmic paths, we do ascend,
Each heartbeat a message we send,
Seeking solace in the vast,
Echoes of love, forever cast.

With open arms, we touch the sky,
Embracing visions that soar high,
In unity, we find our place,
Celestial echoes of His grace.

Through trials faced, we stand as one,
Beneath the warmth of the rising sun,
Our faith ignited, spirits rise,
In the dance of stars, hope never dies.

As dawn awakens, shadows fade,
In light anew, our lives are laid,
Through every moment, love will flow,
In celestial echoes, forever glow.

Lanterns in the Darkness

When shadows stretch and silence reclaims,
We light our lanterns, calling His names,
In every flicker, a promise bright,
Guiding us through the deep of night.

With faith as fuel, we brave the storm,
In the arms of love, we find our form,
Each lantern's glow, a beacon of grace,
Illuminating paths we embrace.

Together we stand, hearts intertwined,
With every challenge, courage aligned,
In the darkest hour, our spirits shine,
Each lantern a whisper of the divine.

Through trials faced and battles won,
In unity, we rise as one,
For in the darkness, our light takes flight,
Lanterns of hope, piercing the night.

So let us shine, with hearts ablaze,
Through every moment, in love we praise,
As lanterns flicker and spirits sing,
In the darkness, His blessing brings.

Light Beyond the Veil

In shadows deep, the spirits call,
Their whispers weave through time's great hall.
A light appears, so warm, so bright,
It guides us home through darkest night.

With each step taken towards the glow,
We find our path, our spirits grow.
The veil is thin, the truth revealed,
In sacred light, our hearts are healed.

Eternal hope, the flame inside,
Through trials faced, we shall abide.
Embrace the grace that now unfolds,
In every story, love retold.

As dawn breaks forth, the shadows flee,
We walk in faith, the light to see.
Our hands uplifted, prayers ascend,
In harmony, our souls shall blend.

So trust the light beyond the veil,
Let love and peace forever sail.
For in this journey, we align,
With every heartbeat, we are divine.

Moments of Holy Illumination

In quiet dawn, the spirit sings,
Awakening dreams, on gentle wings.
Moments of grace, so sweet, so rare,
Illuminate hearts with tender care.

Each breath we take, a sacred gift,
In praise and joy, our spirits lift.
With open hands, we share the light,
A dance of love, in pure delight.

Paths entwined by faith's intention,
In stillness found, our hearts' ascension.
Through trials faced, we learn to grow,
In holy moments, we come to know.

As stars align in velvet skies,
We seek the truth through open eyes.
Each flicker shines, a promise made,
In moments rich, our fears will fade.

So hold this light, let it expand,
With every heartbeat, take a stand.
In moments blessed, forever be,
With holy love, we're truly free.

The Sacred Journal of Radiance

In pages filled with sacred lore,
We write the truths that we adore.
The sacred journal, open wide,
Records our steps, our faith, our pride.

With ink of light, our stories flow,
In every line, our spirits glow.
Reflections bright, of love we share,
In gratitude, we find our prayer.

An odyssey of heart and mind,
In sacred space, our souls unwind.
Each chapter holds a lesson learned,
In radiance, our hearts are turned.

Through trials faced and joys embraced,
In every moment, love is traced.
The journal speaks of paths we've crossed,
In sacred bond, we count no loss.

So let us write with fervent grace,
In every heartbeat, love's embrace.
The sacred journal, forever bright,
A testament of purest light.

Twinkling Promises of the Soul

In the stillness of the night,
Twinkling stars, a guiding light.
Promises whispered on the breeze,
With every breath, our hearts find ease.

Each flicker shines with hope anew,
In dreams that dance, and visions true.
They beckon us to trust the way,
Through trials faced, we shall not sway.

The universe, a sacred weave,
In every thread, we learn to believe.
Through mountain highs and valley lows,
The light within, forever glows.

In symphony, our souls unite,
Connected by the boundless light.
With every twinkle, love awakes,
In sacred bond, our spirit stakes.

So let us walk through cosmic grace,
In every heart, a sacred place.
Twinkling promises of the soul,
In divine unity, we become whole.

In the Shadow of Grace

In the stillness of the night,
We seek Your gentle embrace,
With faith our hearts ignited,
In the shadow of Your grace.

Through trials we find our way,
Your light forever near,
In whispers and in silence,
We feel You drawing near.

With every breath, we praise You,
In the beauty all around,
Let our souls be anchored,
In Your love, we are bound.

Guide us through the darkness,
As stars in heaven gleam,
In the stillness, we surrender,
To the depths of every dream.

In Your mercy, we find hope,
A promise shining bright,
In the shadow of Your whispers,
We rise, renewed in light.

The Dawning Spirit

Awakened by the morning,
A soft and gentle call,
The dawning spirit rises,
And brings forth love for all.

With rays of hope and promise,
Each heart begins to bloom,
In unity, we gather,
To break the bonds of gloom.

The sun spills forth its glory,
On valleys wide and deep,
In nature's grand symphony,
Our souls begin to leap.

Embrace the light within us,
Let kindness be our guide,
Together we will flourish,
With God we will abide.

As the heavens turn to gold,
We shine with joy and grace,
In the dawning spirit's warmth,
We find our sacred place.

Whispers from the Divine

In every breath we take,
There are whispers from the divine,
Echoes of eternal love,
In moments, they intertwine.

Through the rustling of the leaves,
And the songbirds high above,
We hear the gentle guidance,
Of our Creator's love.

Amidst the storms of doubt,
Your assurances ring clear,
In the silent spaces,
You cradle every fear.

In the warmth of sacred silence,
Our souls find sweet release,
With each whisper, You awaken,
A longing for this peace.

May we heed these soft invitations,
With hearts and minds aligned,
In the sacred flow of being,
We are forever entwined.

Illuminated Paths

On paths that stretch before us,
In the light of heaven's grace,
We walk with hope and courage,
In each chosen place.

With every step, we harbor,
The dreams that lift our soul,
In the tapestry of life,
We find our sacred role.

Through valleys dark and winding,
Your guidance is our thread,
In moments lost in shadow,
You lead with love instead.

Each encounter, a reminder,
Of grace that flows like streams,
In the journey, we discover,
The power of our dreams.

As we follow illuminated paths,
With faith, we bravely start,
In every twist and turn,
We carry love in our heart.

The Beacon Within

In the quiet heart, light appears,
Guiding souls through stormy spheres.
Faith ignites the darkest night,
With a spark, we seek the light.

In shadows deep, we find our song,
Whispers of love where we belong.
Hope, the flame that never dims,
Rises high on soaring hymns.

In trials faced, we stand as one,
Holding hands till battles are won.
Together we walk, side by side,
With the spirit as our guide.

The beacon shines, our path made clear,
Through each joy and every tear.
In unity, our hearts will swell,
A radiant truth we long to tell.

Let the inner light break through,
Transforming all in shades anew.
In every soul, a light divine,
Together, we eternally shine.

Ascending Toward Brilliance

With every breath, we rise anew,
Chasing dreams in skies of blue.
Hearts ablaze, we chase the sun,
In every step, our souls will run.

Lifting spirits on the wings,
Joyful cries as heaven sings.
In the heights, our visions gleam,
Fulfilling each and every dream.

Boundless grace, our hearts expand,
Walking forth, hand in hand.
Through the trials, we ascend,
Toward the light that knows no end.

In the silence, wisdom flows,
Nurtured by the love it sows.
With each dawn, new strength arrived,
In brilliance, we shall abide.

Rising higher, we will see,
The sacred truth that sets us free.
Together bright, our spirits soar,
Ascending to forevermore.

Threads of Celestial Hope

In the tapestry of life, we weave,
Threads of dreams that we believe.
Intertwined in love's embrace,
We find our strength, our sacred space.

Each fiber speaks of battles fought,
In moments lost and lessons taught.
With every stitch, we mend the seams,
Crafting worlds from whispered dreams.

Through skies of gray and streams of light,
Hope ignites our darkest night.
In every heart, a purpose blooms,
A gentle hand through all the glooms.

We gather here, though miles apart,
Connected deep, heart to heart.
In unity, our voices raise,
Lifting spirits in wondrous praise.

In the cosmos, our stories thread,
Binding us through what is said.
With every hope, a dream to cast,
Celestial whispers, forever last.

Embracing the Sacred Shine

In silence deep, we hear the call,
To embrace the shine that lights us all.
With open hearts and mindful grace,
We walk together, face to face.

Each sacred moment, pure and bright,
Reflects the love that births the light.
With gratitude, we dance and sing,
In every heart, a sacred spring.

In the stillness, truth unfolds,
Guiding us through paths of gold.
With each sunrise, a brand new chance,
To join the universe's dance.

Holding close what truly matters,
In the love that softly flatters.
Embracing joy and letting go,
In the sacred glow, we steadily grow.

As we shine, we light the way,
For others lost to find their stay.
With love embraced, we boldly shine,
Together in the grand divine.

Tender Rays of Belief

In dawn's soft glow, we find our peace,
As gentle whispers never cease.
Faith rises like the morning sun,
Uniting hearts, we are all one.

Through trials faced, we find our grace,
In every tear, His warm embrace.
With tender rays that guide our way,
We walk in love, come what may.

In sacred silence, prayers take flight,
Illuminated by His light.
Each moment shared, a holy sign,
In boundless love, our spirits shine.

With open hands, we share our song,
A melody where we belong.
Through joy and sorrow, we will tread,
In faith, we rise, in love, we're led.

As stars align in night's embrace,
We seek His truth, a sacred space.
United by the hope we feel,
In tender rays, our hearts reveal.

The Coat of Divine Light

A coat woven from threads of grace,
A shield against life's harshest face.
In moments dark, its glow will rise,
A promise wrapped in azure skies.

With every stitch, His love we weave,
A tapestry that won't deceive.
Through trials worn and burdens bold,
With faith, a warmth against the cold.

Each tear a pearl, each joy a seam,
In unity, we'll dare to dream.
Together clad in colors bright,
We twirl beneath the stars at night.

The coat bestowed upon each heart,
A sacred bond, no soul apart.
In vibrant hues, His spirit glows,
As we embrace the path He shows.

With every heartbeat, love ignites,
A beacon shining through our nights.
In holy whispers, we are told,
The coat of light will never fold.

Oasis of Radiant Truth

In desert sands of doubt and fear,
We seek the oasis, ever near.
With open hearts, we find the stream,
A source of life, a precious dream.

Each drop of faith, a crystal clear,
Refreshing souls who gather here.
In the stillness, wisdom flows,
A holy balm that gently grows.

In nature's arms, we hear His call,
Embracing each, we rise, we fall.
Within this space of love so bright,
We find our path, we find the light.

The palm trees sway, a rhythmic tune,
As sunbeams dance beneath the moon.
In every breeze, His presence felt,
In sacred truths, our hearts melt.

Together gathered, hand in hand,
Within this oasis, we take a stand.
With grateful hearts, we share the gift,
In love's embrace, our spirits lift.

Journey Through Sacred Shadows

In shadows deep, we walk anew,
With guiding light, our visions true.
Through valleys low and mountains steep,
In whispered prayers, our souls we keep.

Each step we take, a chance to grow,
As love illuminates the shadow.
In darkest nights, we'll find our way,
With faith as star, it lights the gray.

Voices echo through the trees,
A symphony upon the breeze.
In sacred silence, hope ignites,
As hearts converge beneath the heights.

Through trials faced and burdens borne,
In every tear, a new dawn's born.
With courage drawn from heaven's grace,
We journey on, time cannot erase.

Together we find strength in strife,
In sacred shadows, we embrace life.
Through every trial, the light remains,
In shadows cast, His love sustains.

The Quiet Call of the Soul

In hush of night, whispers arise,
A gentle urge beneath the skies.
Softly beckons, the heart's embrace,
Seeking solace, a sacred place.

Flickering stars, a guiding light,
In shadows deep, revealing sight.
With every breath, the spirit sings,
In stillness found, the joy it brings.

Awake within, a dance of grace,
Divine essence, a warm trace.
Through quietude, the truth unfolds,
A sacred story, softly told.

From depths unknown, the soul shall soar,
Embraced by love, forevermore.
In solitude, the voices call,
Listen close, the quiet call.

In the silence, we find the way,
To light our hearts, to guide our day.
Each echo sings of what we seek,
In whispers soft, the soul's mystique.

Echoes of the Eternal Bond

In timeless whispers, love resides,
In every heartbeat, faith abides.
With echoes soft, our spirits sing,
In shadows cast, we find our wing.

Together we traverse the skies,
In every star, a love that cries.
Through every trial, hand in hand,
In unity, we take a stand.

The threads of fate, they intertwine,
In sacred spaces, pure and divine.
With every step, a promise made,
In echoes bright, our fears will fade.

In the dance of life, we find our way,
In sacred light, we choose to stay.
With hearts ablaze, we share our song,
In love's embrace, we all belong.

In every moment, we know the truth,
In the depths of love, we find our youth.
With gratitude, we lift our voices,
In eternal bond, our heart rejoices.

Hymns of the Beating Sacred

In the stillness, hearts align,
With rhythms pure, we intertwine.
Voices rise, like incense sweet,
In reverence, our souls repeat.

From dawn to dusk, we seek the light,
Through shadowed paths, we find our sight.
A melody of love, divine,
Guides our steps, a sacred sign.

Each whispered prayer, a gentle stream,
Flows through faith, a holy dream.
Together we stand, hand in hand,
In this offering, we understand.

Lifted high, our spirits soar,
In every heart, a sacred core.
Through trials faced, we find the grace,
In hymns of love, we find our place.

Threads of Faith Intertwined

In tapestry, our lives are spun,
Each thread a story, a journey begun.
Woven close, through joy and pain,
In faith's embrace, we rise again.

With gentle hands, we craft the bond,
Through trials deep, we learn to respond.
In every heart, a silent plea,
Intertwined, we seek to be free.

From whispers soft, to shouts of praise,
We journey forth through life's mysterious maze.
Unity found in diverse voices,
In love's embrace, the heart rejoices.

Each moment shared beneath the sun,
In gathering, our spirits run.
Together we thread, and never part,
In every stitch, a faithful heart.

Beneath the Veil of Grace

In shadows deep, where secrets lie,
A veil of grace, our souls rely.
Through trials faced, we seek the way,
In every dawn, a chance to stay.

Beneath the stars, we find our truth,
In whispered dreams of eternal youth.
With open hearts, we dare to tread,
In pathways where the faithful led.

Each tear that falls, a sacred sign,
In brokenness, the light will shine.
A gentle hand to lift the head,
Beneath the veil, our fears are shed.

Together we walk, through night and day,
In unity, fears drift away.
With trust in grace, we find our peace,
In every step, our doubts release.

Reverent Whispers of Togetherness

In sacred spaces, voices blend,
Each whisper soft, a love to send.
With hearts attuned, we seek the face,
Of divinity in shared embrace.

With open arms, we greet the dawn,
In reverent stillness, we are drawn.
Through trials faced and joys bestowed,
Our unity, a boundless road.

From silent prayers to songs of grace,
In every moment, we find a place.
Together we stand, fierce and bold,
In whispers shared, our truths unfold.

In every tear, a story shared,
In every joy, a heart that cared.
With kindness woven, hand in hand,
In reverence, together we stand.

Guardian Angels of Our Bonds

In shadows deep, our spirits dwell,
With guardian angels, their secrets to tell.
They weave between us, a bond so tight,
Guiding our hearts, a divine light.

Together we rise, through trials and tears,
With every prayer, they calm our fears.
In unity's grace, we find our way,
Blessed by the angels, night and day.

They whisper hope when the world feels cold,
A tapestry of love, in their arms we hold.
With wings of mercy, they shelter our hearts,
In every moment, their guidance never departs.

When paths are lost, and doubts collide,
These angels restore the faith inside.
They carry our wishes, as soft as a dove,
In the shelter of grace, we find our love.

Forever entwined, our spirits take flight,
With guardian angels, we embrace the light.
In the bond that we share, divinely spun,
Together we'll flourish, as one in the sun.

The Spiritual Symphony of Togetherness

In harmony's grace, our souls align,
Together we sing, your heart and mine.
With every note, a sacred tune,
In the spiritual symphony, we are immune.

Resonating softly, through laughter and pain,
Our spirits entwined, as gentle rain.
The melody flows, in whispers and shouts,
A dance of the devout, in love, no doubts.

Each chord we strike, a promise of light,
In the music of unity, we take flight.
With every crescendo, the world fades away,
In the warmth of your presence, I long to stay.

As we weave our dreams, through prayers we share,
The harmony blooms, a fragrant prayer.
In the sanctuary built by our trust,
Together we flourish, in love we must.

In the rhythm, dear sister, brother, and friend,
The spiritual symphony shall never end.
With hearts as the instruments, souls intertwined,
In love's divine music, true peace we find.

Threads of Destiny's Design

In the fabric of life, a thread does weave,
Destiny's design, in hope we believe.
With every stitch, a story unfolds,
A tapestry rich, in colors and golds.

Through moments divine, our paths were spun,
Intertwining souls, together as one.
In laughter, in sorrow, the threads align,
With faith in each other, our hearts combine.

Guided by light, through shadows we tread,
In the patterns of love, divine trust is spread.
As the loom of time weaves day into night,
In our woven lives, we find pure light.

Every twist and turn is a sacred chance,
To dance in the rhythm, the cosmic dance.
Threads may entangle, but they won't break,
In the heart of our love, each choice we make.

With hands intertwined, we honor the thread,
In destiny's embrace, we're softly led.
The fabric of us, forever designed,
In the weft of our journey, true peace we find.

Radiance in Our Sacred Union

In the dawn of love, our spirits ignite,
A radiant glow, pure and bright.
In the sacred union, our vows declared,
With hearts intertwined, the universe shared.

Like stars in the heavens, forever we shine,
In the light of our bond, love so divine.
Through trials and joy, our flame will grow,
In the sacred embrace, we shall sow.

Together we bloom, like flowers in spring,
In the garden of life, our praises we sing.
With every heartbeat, a symphony plays,
In the dance of our love, we find better days.

Through whispers of grace, our path becomes clear,
Hand in hand, love conquers all fear.
In the radiance of truth, our spirits ascend,
In this sacred union, there's no end.

Together we stand, in the warmth of the sun,
In the light of our love, we are forever one.
In this sacred journey, hand in heart we'll go,
Radiance in our union, a celestial glow.

The Alchemy of Love's Spirit

In the silence of the dawn's embrace,
Resplendent light begins to chase,
Whispers of grace in every heart,
Binding us close, never apart.

Each tear a pearl in the ocean's vast,
Reflections of love from ages past,
Through trials we rise, like phoenix in flight,
Transforming darkness into radiant light.

In the prayer of a humble soul,
The alchemy makes us truly whole,
With every step on this sacred path,
We find the joy amid the wrath.

The essence of love, a priceless gold,
In gentle hands, the gifts unfold,
From the furnace of faith, we learn and grow,
Sharing the light, in ebb and flow.

So grasp this spirit like morning dew,
Let it guide your heart, pure and true,
For in love's alchemy, we discern,
Beauty eternal, from which we learn.

Harmonies of the Boundless Heart

In the quiet, where souls intertwine,
Harmonies rise, a sacred sign,
Songs of peace dance in the air,
Uniting hearts with tender care.

Where shadows fall, love's lanterns gleam,
Awakening hearts, igniting the dream,
Each note aligned in a divine accord,
Filling the silence, with love restored.

The infinite whispers through the trees,
Breezes carrying ancient decrees,
In every heartbeat, the truth we find,
Connection divine, transcending time.

With arms open wide, embrace the call,
In the symphony, we rise or fall,
Together we weave this celestial quilt,
With threads of compassion, love's purest silt.

Let every soul sing this sacred song,
Unified spirits, we all belong,
For in the harmonies of the boundless heart,
We find the magic that sets us apart.

Devotional Threads of the Infinite

In each prayer, a thread is spun,
Connecting earth to the heavens run,
With hands uplifted, we weave our fate,
In devotion, love cannot wait.

The infinite whispers through the night,
Guiding the lost toward the light,
Each act of kindness, a stitch in time,
Weaving our lives, a holy rhyme.

Through challenges faced, we grow and learn,
In the heat of the furnace, faith will burn,
With every heartbeat, a sacred vow,
In this journey, we learn how.

Threads of compassion join us as one,
Beneath the gaze of the eternal sun,
In every moment, love's touch we feel,
Binding us closer, our souls reveal.

So take a breath and feel the grace,
In this tapestry, we find our place,
For devotional threads, though unseen,
Connect us all to the Divine's dream.

Whispers Across the Celestial Divide

In the stillness, a calling clear,
Soft whispers carry, drawing near,
Echoes of love that span the skies,
Uniting souls where the spirit flies.

Across the vastness, beyond the stars,
Hearts make pilgrimage, transcending bars,
In the silence, we hear the song,
Of ancient wisdom that guides us along.

When burdens weigh heavy on our souls,
Lifted by faith, love makes us whole,
Each whisper a promise, a tender grace,
Bringing us back to the sacred space.

With every prayer, a bowing heart,
In the cosmic dance, we play our part,
In the intimacy of dusk and dawn,
We find our strength, and we carry on.

So listen closely for the divine note,
In the everyday, love we promote,
For whispers across the celestial sea,
Remind us forever, we are free.

Prayerful Weavings of Destiny

In shadows deep, we seek the light,
Our hearts entwined, a sacred rite.
With whispered hopes on breath of prayer,
We find our strength, we cast our care.

Each step we take, a guiding star,
In paths unknown, though near and far.
The threads of faith, a tapestry,
Unraveled love, our destiny.

Together we rise, hand in hand,
Through trials faced, we understand.
In silent vows, our spirits blend,
A holy bond that will not end.

Seek not the sights of worldly gain,
But treasures found through joy and pain.
The purpose clear, our spirits soar,
In prayerful weavings, we implore.

Let echoes swell, with voices bright,
In unity, we shine our light.
As destinies weave, we stand as one,
A fragrant bloom beneath the sun.

Devotions in Silent Spheres

In hushed repose, we bow our heads,
To seek the truth where silence spreads.
With gentle hearts, we feel the call,
In sacred stillness, we find our all.

Each moment holds a sacred grace,
In quietude, we seek His face.
The spheres of spirit softly hum,
A symphony of peace begun.

We breathe in faith, our souls align,
With every pulse, divine design.
In whispered thoughts, the heavens speak,
In holy devotions, strong yet meek.

From silent depths, our prayers arise,
A bridge to Him, beyond the skies.
In every heart, His love abides,
In sacred vows, our truth resides.

Through stillness found, we learn to see,
The sacred weave of destiny.
In realms unknown, our spirits soar,
Devotions offered evermore.

The Choir of Unified Hearts

With voices raised in harmony,
We gather here, as one decree.
In notes of love, our spirits blend,
A choir formed, where hopes ascend.

Each heart a note, in grand design,
Together we sing, a holy line.
In melodies that break all chains,
We forge connections, love remains.

Through trials faced and burdens shared,
A symphony, divinely prepared.
In unity, our spirits meet,
The choir of hearts, where souls are sweet.

As chords resound, our faith ignites,
In sacred space, we find our might.
With every song, our spirits rise,
In harmony, we touch the skies.

Let rhythms flow, through every tear,
In joyous songs, we draw Him near.
With hope declared and love imparted,
A choir of hearts, forever started.

Communion in the Divine

In sacred moments, time stands still,
We gather close, by choice, by will.
With humble hearts, we seek to find,
Communion deep, in love entwined.

The essence shared, a holy bond,
In every breath, our souls respond.
In grace bestowed, we lift our praise,
In shared communion, love ablaze.

Each prayer a tender, soft embrace,
An opening to His boundless space.
In every heart, a sacred glow,
Communion flows, both fast and slow.

With eyes uplifted, spirits rise,
In joyful hearts, we reach the skies.
Through sacred ties, we find our way,
In communion, night gives way to day.

In every gathering, love's refrain,
A tapestry of joy and pain.
Together, we find what is divine,
In communion, our souls align.

A Pilgrimage of Heartfelt Convergence

Through valleys wide, our spirits roam,
In search of truth, we find our home.
Each path we tread, a step in grace,
In sacred shrouds, we seek His face.

Under starlit skies, we lift our prayer,
With every heartbeat, we declare.
Embraced by love, we feel the light,
Together we rise, dispelling night.

In whispered winds, the answers dwell,
Guided by faith, our souls compel.
A pilgrimage shared, through trials we pave,
A journey defined by the One who saves.

With hands entwined, we bear the load,
Across the fields, we walk this road.
The heart of man, a sacred space,
Where all are welcomed by His grace.

As dawn breaks forth, we greet the day,
With hearts ablaze, we sing and pray.
In unity, we forge a bond,
A pilgrimage where we respond.

Hymns Penned by the Divine

In quiet corners, voices rise,
A symphony beneath the skies.
With every breath, a sacred note,
In harmony, our spirits float.

Each hymn unfurls, a gentle breeze,
Whispers of love in ancient trees.
The melodies curling, soft and pure,
In hearts of many, they endure.

Beneath the arch of heaven's dome,
We find our place, we make our home.
With every song, His love proclaimed,
Through trials faced, we are unchained.

In sacred rhythms, hope reclaims,
Our voices echo in His name.
Together we gather, side by side,
In faith's embrace, our hearts abide.

From mountains high to oceans wide,
The hymns we sing, a sacred guide.
In unity we find the way,
As one, we rise to greet the day.

Communion of Kindred Spirits

In circles drawn, our hearts align,
With quiet strength, our souls entwine.
Through laughter shared and tears that flow,
In kindred bonds, our spirits grow.

The stories told, the hands we clasp,
In gentle hugs, salvation grasp.
Through trials faced, together we stand,
With love's embrace, we understand.

In every echoed prayer, we find,
A common thread that binds our mind.
With shared beliefs, we rise as one,
In unity, our race is run.

The spirit dances among us here,
With every word, we draw Him near.
In sacred communion, hearts awake,
In joyful bonds, new paths we make.

As kindred spirits, we shall soar,
In faith's embrace, forevermore.
With open hearts, we kindle light,
Together we journey toward the light.

The Fount of Compassionate Ties

From deepest wells, compassion flows,
In every heart, a garden grows.
With nurturing hands, we plant the seeds,
In every soul, love gently feeds.

Through open arms, we share the weight,
In kindness given, we find our fate.
The fount of grace that binds us tight,
Illuminates our darkest night.

In humble service, we find our joy,
For every girl and every boy.
With gentle touches, we heal the sore,
In love's embrace, we open doors.

The ties we weave, a sacred thread,
In life's tapestry, love is spread.
With every tear, we offer hope,
Together as one, we find our scope.

As rivers flow, our hearts abide,
Through every struggle, love's our guide.
In compassionate ties, we grow as one,
Forever shining like the sun.

Sacred Echoes of the Soul

In the quiet of dusk's embrace,
Whispers of grace begin to trace.
Every heartbeat sings divine,
In sacred echoes, our spirits align.

Light reflects on paths we tread,
Guided by truths that gently wed.
Hope flickers in shadows deep,
In sacred echoes, our promises keep.

Through valleys where darkness looms,
Love's gentle light forever blooms.
With each prayer, a star takes flight,
In sacred echoes, we find our light.

Voices of angels softly call,
In moments still, we hear them all.
Their melodies cradle our souls,
In sacred echoes, we are made whole.

Let the journey lead us near,
To a place where love draws clear.
In unity, our spirits rise,
In sacred echoes, eternity lies.

Celestial Whispers of Longing

Stars twinkle like dreams yet to find,
Celestial whispers beckon the mind.
In the stillness of night's embrace,
We seek the touch of sacred grace.

Hearts ache with a yearning profound,
For the presence of love all around.
In tears we plant seeds of hope,
Celestial whispers teach us to cope.

Every prayer lifts us high,
Carried forth, like birds to the sky.
In the silence, the spirit breathes,
Celestial whispers weave love in wreathes.

With each dawn, we rise anew,
Drawing strength from the holy view.
In longing, we discover our song,
Celestial whispers remind us we belong.

Together, hearts will find their way,
Beyond the shadows of yesterday.
In unity, we flourish and grow,
Celestial whispers guide us to know.

The Tapestry of Devotion

Threads of faith entwine as one,
Woven tightly, hope has begun.
In every stitch, a story told,
The tapestry of love we hold.

Colors blend, and shadows dance,
In devotion, we find our chance.
Each moment, a thread to share,
The tapestry of grace laid bare.

In trials faced, our strength is found,
With each knot, a bond unbound.
Together, we craft our way,
The tapestry of night and day.

With hands that give, and hearts that feel,
In devotion, our spirits heal.
Every prayer, a golden hue,
The tapestry of love shines through.

As the fabric stretches wide,
Faith unites, and hope won't hide.
In every heart, a place to belong,
The tapestry of life sings strong.

Faith's Fragile Ties

In whispers soft, our fears arise,
Faith's fragile ties, a sweet disguise.
Through tempest's roar and stormy night,
We cling to love, our guiding light.

Each worry, like a fleeting breath,
In faith's embrace, we conquer death.
With open hearts, we learn to trust,
Faith's fragile ties bind us like dust.

In moments where doubt tries to sway,
Love's fragile ties will light the way.
Through trials faced, we grow so strong,
Faith's fragile ties help us along.

Patience weaves through every prayer,
A promise made, forever fair.
In vulnerability, we stand tall,
Faith's fragile ties uplift us all.

So let the world bring fears untold,
In faith's embrace, we find our gold.
Together bound, our hearts will soar,
Faith's fragile ties forevermore.

The Infinite Circle of Yaleach

In quiet whispers, secrets dwell,
The paths of fate, we cannot quell.
With open hearts, we seek the light,
In Yaleach's arms, we reunite.

The stars above, they guide our flight,
Through shadows deep, we find our sight.
Each step we take, a sacred dance,
In woven dreams, our souls expanse.

The river flows, with timeless grace,
Reflecting love in every space.
In every tear and every smile,
We join the circle, mile by mile.

The sun will rise, the moon will wane,
Through joy and sorrow, love remains.
With hands held tight, we spiral on,
In Yaleach's circle, we are one.

So let us cherish each embrace,
In unity, we find our place.
The infinite circle draws us near,
In harmony, we cast all fear.

Love's Pilgrim Path to the Divine

With every step, we seek the grace,
In love's embrace, we find our place.
Through valleys low, and mountains high,
We journey forth, with hearts awry.

The pilgrim's path, a winding way,
Through trials faced, we learn to sway.
In every shadow, light will gleam,
In love's sweet whisper, we will dream.

The songs of old, they guide our feet,
In sacred rhythm, our hearts beat.
With open arms, we greet the dawn,
On love's path, we are reborn.

As stars adorn the evening sky,
We lift our voices, soaring high.
In every prayer, in every sigh,
We touch the divine, we know no lie.

So let us walk, hand in hand,
With faith and hope, together stand.
On love's pilgrim path, we find delight,
In sacred union, pure and bright.

The Eternal Flame of Unity

In every heart, a flame does burn,
A light of love, for which we yearn.
Through trials faced, and sorrows shared,
In unity, we are prepared.

Together strong, we stand as one,
Beneath the moon, beneath the sun.
Our souls entwined, in bonds so deep,
In every promise, we shall keep.

The flame of hope, it flickers bright,
Guiding us through the darkest night.
In every gesture, every deed,
We sow the love, the world does need.

With every spark, a dream ignites,
In unity, we reach new heights.
Through love's embrace, we break the chains,
In every heart, eternity reigns.

So let us cherish what we find,
In the eternal flame, we're intertwined.
Together we shine, with love so true,
In unity's light, we start anew.

The Covenant of Love's Embrace

In the garden of grace we stand,
Bound together by a guiding hand.
Hearts entwined in sacred trust,
Promised forever, in love we must.

Through trials fierce and shadows cast,
Our faith shall hold, our spirits steadfast.
With whispers soft, we share our souls,
In every breath, our love consoles.

Upon the altar of dreams we lay,
With hope and joy, we find our way.
Light shines bright in the darkest night,
In Love's embrace, we find our light.

Together we seek the path divine,
With every heartbeat, your hand in mine.
An everlasting vow we make,
For in each moment, love shall awake.

Seraphic Bonds of Tenderness

In soft whispers, angels sing,
Embracing hearts, to love they cling.
Wings spread wide, blessings descend,
In tender bonds, our souls transcend.

Through trials faced, and storms we know,
Yet still the seeds of kindness grow.
In every touch, a spark divine,
With each embrace, our spirits shine.

With gentle grace, we heal the pain,
In love's pure light, we break the chain.
A dance of joy, a life's embrace,
Together we find our sacred space.

In every prayer, our hopes arise,
As we behold each other's eyes.
With every heartbeat, love's refrain,
In seraph's bonds, we will remain.

Transcendent Melodies of the Heart

In silence deep, our spirits soar,
Melodies of love forevermore.
In harmony, our souls align,
Transcendent songs, divinely fine.

The symphony of grace we share,
Echoes softly on the air.
Each note a promise, pure and sweet,
In love's embrace, our hearts do beat.

With every chord, we lift our praise,
Through trials faced, in endless days.
In every tear, a song is spun,
In melodies, we are as one.

Sing out the truth, let love be known,
In every heart, His light has shone.
Together we weave this sacred art,
Transcendent melodies of the heart.

Reverence in the Silken Ties

In silken ties, our lives entwined,
A reverence for love, divinely designed.
With every breath, a prayer we share,
In sacred grace, we find our prayer.

Through trials' storm, we rise above,
Anchored solid in endless love.
With gentle hands, we weave our fate,
In reverent silence, we communicate.

Each moment cherished, a treasure rare,
In the warmth of your presence, we're laid bare.
Together we step on this sacred ground,
In love's embrace, our joy is found.

With faith as our guide, we journey far,
Embracing the light, our guiding star.
In silken ties, our hearts shall bloom,
In reverence, we dispel the gloom.

Luminescence in Sacred Kinship

In the hush of dawn's light, we gather wide,
Hearts entwined, with faith as our guide.
Voices meld in harmony, a sacred song,
Together we stand, where we all belong.

Threads of love weave a tapestry bright,
Each soul a beacon, casting pure light.
In moments of silence, our spirits unite,
Shadows disperse, revealing the might.

In trials we find the strength to endure,
With hands clasped tight, our hearts are sure.
Together we walk this divine path,
Embracing the journey, feeling the bath.

In the twilight, prayers rise like smoke,
Binding our hopes, the future awoke.
With gratitude vibrant, we honor the past,
In sacred kinship, our bonds hold fast.

As stars twinkle softly in night's embrace,
We seek His wisdom, our hearts find grace.
In every whisper, His love we see,
Luminescence guiding you and me.

The Unseen Ties of Faith

In the silence, we find a gentle touch,
A faith unseen, yet cherished so much.
Threads of belief weave an endless chain,
Bringing us comfort in joy and in pain.

As seasons change and time flows on,
The ties grow stronger; our fears are gone.
In every prayer, a heart beats deep,
Together in spirit, our promises we keep.

Through storms and trials, we rise anew,
Bound by a love that carries us through.
In the quiet moments, we stand as one,
Illuminated brightly, like the morning sun.

With every challenge, we gather near,
Faith in our hearts, we cast out the fear.
With hands raised up, in unity we seek,
The unseen ties that bring strength to the weak.

Together we witness the miracles unfold,
In stories of old, and the new yet untold.
Trusting the path, as we faithfully tread,
In the unseen ties, the spirit is fed.

The Covenant of Togetherness

Upon this ground, we take a stand,
With open hearts, and joined hands.
In the sacred bond of every soul,
We find the purpose that makes us whole.

Within the circle, love does flow,
In laughter and tears, it starts to grow.
Each voice a note in this symphony,
Together we rise, in sweet harmony.

In the depth of darkness, we shine so bright,
A guiding star in the deepest night.
From the ashes of sorrow, we bloom like a rose,
In the covenant of togetherness, love eternally grows.

As dawn breaks forth with promises new,
We cherish the moments as life's hues.
Each lesson learned, each story told,
In the covenant, our spirits unfold.

With faith as the compass, we navigate wide,
In togetherness, there's nothing to hide.
In joy and in struggle, we hold each tight,
A sacred blessing in the love-filled light.

Enchanted Pedals of Reverence

In gardens of faith, we softly tread,
With enchanted petals, our spirits are fed.
Each bloom a prayer, vibrant and true,
Whispers of grace from me to you.

Beneath the sky, where the soft winds play,
We gather in peace to honor the day.
With every petal, we share our song,
In the symphony of life, we all belong.

As nature unfolds her sacred might,
We find our solace in the morning light.
In every color, divine love shines,
Gently reminding us that hope entwines.

Through seasons' changes, with every breath,
We cherish the beauty that conquers death.
In enchanted petals, we find our way,
With reverence guiding, come what may.

With hearts uplifted, we celebrate grace,
In moments of stillness, we find our place.
In the dance of existence, love's gentle thread,
Enchanted pedals of reverence spread.

Divine Threads of Affection

In the stillness of dawn's soft light,
Whispers of love take gentle flight.
Hearts entwined in sacred grace,
Finding solace in His embrace.

Every tear, a prayer sent high,
Each joy shared, a sweet goodbye.
Through trials faced and shadows cast,
Faith's pure thread holds us steadfast.

Within the storm, a quiet peace,
From His love, our fears release.
Bound by promise, hearts ignite,
In the darkness, we find light.

Woven dreams in stars above,
Guiding paths with tender love.
Divine hands shape each fate,
In His timing, we await.

In every breath, His essence flows,
In every heart, His glory grows.
A tapestry of faith we weave,
In His truth, we all believe.

Celestial Bonds Weaving Souls

As the moonlight paints the sea,
Eternal bonds call unto me.
Light and shadow dance anew,
In His name, our spirits flew.

Threads of starlight cross the night,
Binding hearts in pure delight.
Gathered souls in sacred space,
We behold His loving face.

Each step taken, guided hands,
In the silence, love expands.
Voices rise in harmony,
Woven deep in unity.

Through the chaos, peace prevails,
Hope unbroken, love never fails.
Together we shall boldly stand,
With faith found in His command.

Celestial paths lead us home,
Where love's light no longer roams.
In His laughter, sorrow flees,
United in His mysteries.

The Prayer of Silent Embrace

In the quiet of the night,
Hearts whisper prayers in soft light.
Seeking solace, we extend,
In His grace, our spirits mend.

With each heartbeat, we confess,
In stillness, we find His rest.
Voices soft, a sacred sound,
In His love, we are unbound.

Hands uplifted, spirits soar,
Giving thanks forevermore.
Each embrace, a promise made,
In His arms, we are remade.

Seek His wisdom, gentle guide,
In the shadows, He'll abide.
Through the storm, we walk with grace,
In the warmth of love's embrace.

Every moment, divine and blessed,
In our hearts, His peace shall rest.
Through the silence, hear His call,
In His love, we stand tall.

Sacred Echoes of Love

In the dawn, His light shall break,
Echoing love, the earth shall wake.
In every whisper, grace resounds,
As in Heaven, joy abounds.

Together we gather in prayer,
In His presence, burdens rare.
Hands intertwined, hope's embrace,
Every heart finds its place.

Melodies of love we hum,
In the silence, faith will come.
Beneath the stars, we unite,
In this stillness, there is light.

Voices lifted, spirits soar,
In His love, we seek for more.
Each moment, a blessing bestowed,
On this sacred path, we strode.

In the echoes, hear the song,
Of the faithful, proud and strong.
With each heartbeat, love shall call,
In His embrace, we are all.

Love's Celestial Pilgrimage

In the realm where spirits soar,
Hearts entwined forevermore.
Guided by a gentle light,
They traverse the endless night.

Each step a dance of grace,
Finding peace in a sacred place.
The stars whisper their names,
In love's eternal frames.

With faith, they walk the path,
Embracing joy and holy wrath.
Through trials, their souls ignite,
A flame that burns ever bright.

United in a sacred vow,
They blossom in the here and now.
Together they dream and strive,
In this pilgrimage, they thrive.

So let the heavens sing,
Of the love that faith can bring.
In the sacred bond they find,
The truth that binds all mankind.

Sacred Garden of Interwoven Dreams

Beneath the arch of starlit grace,
A garden blooms in time and space.
Where dreams entwine with whispered prayer,
In sacred soil, a love laid bare.

Each flower holds a story long,
In fragrant petals, voices strong.
The roots of faith dive deep and wide,
In the heart where hopes abide.

Gentle breezes wrap around,
Carrying blessings, peace abound.
In every shadow, light will play,
Transforming night into the day.

With every prayer, the blossoms rise,
Reflecting truth within the skies.
In unity, their colors blend,
A testament that hearts can mend.

So wander here, O cherished soul,
Let this sacred place make you whole.
In the interwoven dreams, we see,
A glimpse of love's eternity.

Epistles of Yearning Souls

In silence deep, two hearts converse,
Their whispers penned in verses terse.
Each letter filled with longing eyes,
In ink of truth, no room for lies.

With every sigh, their spirits weave,
Unseen threads of love, they believe.
Across the miles, their souls entwine,
In pages worn, their fates align.

The distance may expand the dream,
Yet hope shall be their steadfast beam.
Through trials faced, their voices blend,
In letters shared, their souls ascend.

Oh yearning hearts, do not despair,
In each epistle, silent prayer.
For love shall guide their trembling hands,
To meet again on sacred lands.

So let the ink of faith stay true,
In every word, a love anew.
For in the ache, the joy will flow,
In epistles of the hearts that know.

The Covenant of Celestial Love

In heavenly halls, a promise made,
Two souls unite, their fears allayed.
With starlit eyes and hearts aligned,
A covenant of love defined.

Bound by grace, they rise above,
In sacred trust, they nurture love.
With every breath, a vow renewed,
In unity, their strength imbued.

Beyond the reach of time and space,
In every trial, they find their place.
For love, a grace that never wanes,
Transforms their joys and eases pains.

Through laughter shared and tears released,
Their journey's path, forever pieced.
Hand in hand, they walk the way,
In the covenant of love, they stay.

So let the heavens bless their tale,
Of love that conquers, will prevail.
In every heartbeat, every sigh,
A celestial bond that will not die.

The Covenant of Kindred Spirits

In sacred bonds, we find our place,
With hearts entwined, we share our grace.
The light of faith does guide our way,
Through trials faced, we shall not sway.

Together we rise, in unity's name,
To honor love, and fan the flame.
With every prayer, our spirits soar,
Connected deep, forevermore.

Through storm and sun, our covenant stands,
With whispered hopes and clasped hands.
A tapestry woven, bright and true,
In kindred hearts, our love renews.

We share a song, of ages past,
In every echo, our truths hold fast.
Divine reflections in each gaze,
In every moment, hear the praise.

Let kindness be our guiding star,
In every distance, near or far.
In sacred trust, we journey on,
The covenant thrives; we are reborn.

Heavenly Resonance of Longing

In dreams we touch, where souls align,
A yearning echo, pure, divine.
Across the veil, our spirits call,
In love's embrace, we shall not fall.

The stars weep light, each distant shine,
With whispered hopes, our hearts entwine.
An ache for unity, deep as the sea,
In heavenly realms, we long to be.

With hearts aflame, we seek the sky,
In sacred silence, hear our cry.
Eternal bonds, unbroken ties,
In longing's grasp, our spirits rise.

Through trials faced, and burdens shared,
In every prayer, our love declared.
As shadows loom, our light will gleam,
In heavenly praise, we'll find our dream.

The hands of fate guide every breath,
In love's embrace, we conquer death.
For in this dance, our souls grow strong,
In heavenly resonance, we belong.

The Divine Connection of Souls

In sacred trust, our spirits blend,
A holy bond that will not end.
With every glance, a silent vow,
In the present moment, here and now.

From distant shores, to hearts so close,
In love's embrace, we find our dose.
With faith as compass, we navigate,
The divine connection shall not wait.

In shared whispers, our truths unfold,
A tapestry of stories bold.
With every heartbeat, we shall know,
This sacred tie continues to grow.

Through trials faced and joys embraced,
In every tear, we find our grace.
The light of truth, our guiding star,
In the divine connection, near or far.

Let laughter ring, let sorrow sway,
In unity's warmth, we shall not stray.
With open hearts, we brave the night,
The divine in us ignites the light.

Sacrosanct Ties of Unity

In every heart, a sacred flame,
With whispered words, we call His name.
The ties we share, they hold us tight,
In unity's bond, we find our light.

Through laughter shared and sorrow's grace,
In every moment, find our place.
With open arms, we rise above,
In sacrosanct ties, we find our love.

When shadows creep, and doubts ignite,
In trusted friendships, we seek the light.
In every prayer, a mirror shines,
In unity's dance, our spirit twines.

The strength we build in faith and trust,
In every challenge, rise we must.
For in this journey, hand in hand,
The ties of unity firmly stand.

Let hope adorn our every step,
In joyful peace, we take our prep.
With hearts as one, in love's embrace,
We weave our dreams in sacred space.

Enkindled by Grace's Caress

In quiet whispers, blessings flow,
Heaven's light guides where we go.
Hearts aflame with love divine,
In grace's hold, our spirits shine.

Through trials faced, we stand as one,
Each step, a song, our journey begun.
With hands held tight, we rise above,
Embraced forever in perfect love.

With prayerful hearts, we seek the light,
In unity's glow, dispelling night.
Together we breathe, in peace we find,
Whispers of faith that bound our minds.

In every moment, grace restores,
Opening wide redemption's doors.
In silence shared, our souls ignite,
This sacred bond, our guiding light.

May love abound in every heart,
In grace's dance, we'll never part.
For in this life, through joy and strife,
We're enkindled by grace, a blessed life.

Echoes of the Sacred Heart

In stillness breathes the sacred sound,
Through beating hearts, our hope is found.
Each echo sings of love's embrace,
An ancient song, our saving grace.

With open arms, He calls us near,
To find our strength, to cast off fear.
In every prayer, our souls unite,
Guided by faith, we seek the light.

Mysterious whispers in the night,
Lead us towards eternal light.
With every heartbeat, we reclaim,
The echoes call us by His name.

Through storms that rage and skies that weep,
The sacred heart in silence keeps.
Through valleys low, and mountains high,
With faith renewed, we will not die.

So let us rise, with voices strong,
In harmony, we find our song.
Echoes of love, a vibrant start,
Together weaving every heart.

The Divine Resonance of Togetherness

In the tapestry of life we weave,
Threads of love that never leave.
In harmony, our spirits sing,
To the joy that together brings.

With every step on this blessed road,
We share each burden, lightening load.
In laughter's grace and gentle tears,
We find the strength that conquers fears.

Hearts in prayer, our souls align,
In sacred space, our lives entwine.
Through trials faced with courage bold,
We rise like phoenixes, hearts of gold.

In moments shared, love's essence flows,
From the divine where mercy grows.
As one we stand, through thick and thin,
Together bound, we always win.

May our unity be ever bright,
A guiding star in darkest night.
For in togetherness, we know,
The divine resonance will always glow.

Celestial Bonds of Hope

In every star, a promise gleams,
Reflecting dreams and sacred themes.
Celestial whispers fill the night,
With bonds of hope, our souls take flight.

Across the skies, the heavens sing,
Of love eternal, light they bring.
In every heartbeat, hope endures,
A grace-filled dance that love ensures.

Through trials faced and sorrows shared,
In shared lament, our spirits bared.
With every tear, a testament,
To love's resolve, our hearts content.

In unity, we find our voice,
With faith as strong, we make our choice.
To lift each other, rise above,
Awash in waves of heavenly love.

May hope resound in every soul,
In celestial light, we all are whole.
Together we dream, together we cope,
In the arms of grace, we find our hope.

The Symphony of Boundless Affection

In the garden where love abounds,
Celestial whispers fill the air.
A symphony of hearts resounds,
In unity, we find our prayer.

Every soul a note in harmony,
Together, we compose our song.
The essence of divinity,
In every beat, we all belong.

Flowing rivers of compassion,
Waves of grace embrace the shore.
In this sacred congregation,
We find strength forevermore.

Each moment, echoes of pure light,
Illuminating paths divine.
In the stillness of the night,
The symphony is yours and mine.

Together, we shall rise above,
In joy and peace, we'll always stand.
Boundless is this sacred love,
A gift from His most gentle hand.

The Spirit's Dance of Convergence

In twilight's glow, the spirits twirl,
Dancing softly, hand in hand.
Each step a moment, love unfurls,
In the light of the sacred land.

With every spin, the world unites,
In harmony, all hearts entwined.
A melody of holy sights,
Where heaven's grace is intertwined.

Through realms unseen, our souls align,
Connected by an endless thread.
The spirit's pulse, a sacred sign,
In every beat, his love is spread.

Let the music guide our flight,
Beyond the shadows, into the sun.
In this dance, all wrongs make right,
As one, we've only just begun.

In the stillness, whispers soar,
A dance that never knows an end.
In this spirit, we implore,
To embrace all as our friend.

Resplendent Tapestries of Love

Threads of gold and silver weave,
In every heart, a story spun.
A tapestry, we do believe,
Reflecting light from everyone.

Each pattern tells of joy and pain,
A vibrant dance of fate combined.
Through trials, love shall ever reign,
In unity, our souls aligned.

Embrace the colors, wide and bold,
Each hue a testament of grace.
In every heart, a truth unfolds,
In every tear, a sacred space.

Together, we will share the thread,
With hands united, we create.
In love's embrace, we forge ahead,
Resplendent in our destined fate.

As one, we weave this sacred art,
In every stitch, a guiding light.
A masterpiece from every heart,
In love's design, all things unite.

Unity in the Face of the Divine

Here we stand before the grace,
In unity, we lift our voice.
Bound by faith, we find our place,
In every heart, the light rejoice.

The heavens watch as we unite,
A chorus of the pure and brave.
In love and truth, we shine so bright,
Facing storms, our souls we save.

With open arms, we greet the day,
In reverence, we are reborn.
Together, we shall find our way,
In the heart where love is worn.

Through trials that may come our path,
In trust, we stand with hearts on fire.
In the face of all that wrath,
We find our strength, we find our choir.

As one we rise, as one we strive,
In faith, we'll carry love's design.
Finding peace in being alive,
Together, we are truly divine.

Bonds Wrought by Divine Hands

In twilight's glow, hearts align,
Sealed by whispers, soft and fine.
A tapestry of grace unveiled,
In sacred trust, our souls are hailed.

The heavens sigh with love's refrain,
Guiding us through joy and pain.
Each moment shared, a holy spark,
Illuminating paths through dark.

With every prayer, our spirits rise,
Bound by faith, we touch the skies.
In every tear, a promise we find,
Together in spirit, our souls entwined.

Through trials faced and storms endured,
In fellowship, our hope assured.
A bond that neither time nor fate,
Can sever or bring to a weight.

So let our hearts be open wide,
With love that flows, a sacred tide.
In Divine hands, we find our song,
A harmony where we belong.

Ethereal Hymns of Affection

In the stillness of the night,
Echoes of love take their flight.
Chanting softly, stars align,
In the heavens, a grand design.

Voices rise, a sweet duet,
In perfect unity, we met.
With every note, a sacred blend,
In harmony that will not end.

Gentle breezes carry grace,
Whispering truths in every place.
In every heart, a song we share,
A melody that fills the air.

With open arms, we gather near,
In peace we've found, casting out fear.
The light of love shall guide the way,
Eternal hymns we sing and play.

Together in this endless flight,
We're bound by love, in holy light.
In ethereal dreams, we dance and sway,
In affection's voice, forever stay.

Light of the Spirit's Embrace

In morning's dawn, your light breaks through,
A gentle warmth that feels so true.
With open hearts, we seek your grace,
In every moment, a sweet embrace.

The spirit whispers, softly near,
Guiding us through doubt and fear.
In trials faced, we feel your hand,
In every step, we understand.

Your love, a beacon, shining clear,
In darkness found, you hold us dear.
Radiance that calls us home,
In spirit's light, we are not alone.

In gratitude, our voices rise,
Joined together, as one we strive.
For in your embrace, we are reborn,
Into the light of a brand new morn.

As life unfolds, we cherish all,
In every rise, in every fall.
With every heartbeat, we embrace,
The light of love in spirit's grace.

Threads Woven in Grace

With every thread, a story spun,
In life's great weave, we are as one.
A quilt of faith, both strong and bright,
In every stitch, our love ignites.

Colors blend, and patterns form,
In life's rich tapestry, we transform.
From joys to sorrows, laughter's song,
Each woven thread, where we belong.

In sacred spaces, hearts connect,
A bond of love, no time can wreck.
Together in this dance we twine,
In every moment, love divine.

Through trials faced, and mountains climbed,
In every fold, our lives entwined.
Threads of grace that cannot break,
In holy union, we awake.

So let us cherish every seam,
In woven tales, we find our dream.
For in this craft of hearts embraced,
We see the beauty, threads of grace.

Illuminated Pathways of Affection

Upon the hills where shadows fade,
Love's gentle light begins to cascade.
Hearts entwined in divine embrace,
Guided by faith, we find our place.

In moments tender, whispers flow,
Echoes of grace, soft and slow.
Each step a blessing, a sacred art,
Uniting souls, never to part.

Through trials faced, we rise as one,
Beneath the watchful eye of the sun.
With every heartbeat, we touch the divine,
In the garden of love, our spirits align.

Hand in hand, we walk the path,
Beside the stream, beyond the wrath.
In prayerful silence, we seek the light,
Illuminated pathways, guiding our sight.

Together we shine, like stars above,
In the tapestry woven from boundless love.
Our journeys vast, in harmony tread,
Each step a promise of joy ahead.

Prayers Entwined in the Soul's Fabric

In the silence where spirits meet,
Foundations built on love's heartbeat.
Every prayer, a thread so fine,
Weaving hearts in faith divine.

Beneath the skies, our wishes soar,
Echoing softly from shore to shore.
In unity, our voices blend,
Prayers entwined, love knows no end.

A sacred bond, unbreakable grace,
Carved in the depths of time and space.
With open hearts, we seek and find,
The fabric of hope, so beautifully aligned.

Each whisper a promise, each tear a light,
Guiding us gently through darkest night.
In the tapestry woven with love's thread,
We rise, we flourish, where angels tread.

Forever upheld by a force so pure,
In the heart's embrace, we stand secure.
With every prayer, our spirits unite,
Entwined in the fabric, ever so bright.

The Sanctuary of Blissful Union

In the sanctuary where spirits dance,
We gather together, a blessed chance.
With whispered prayers and hearts aglow,
In unity's haven, love's river flows.

Each moment cherished, each laugh a song,
In the embrace of love, we all belong.
With open arms, we welcome grace,
In blissful union, we find our place.

Beneath the stars, our dreams take flight,
In the warmth of togetherness, pure delight.
We carry each other, hearts entwined,
In the sanctuary of love, our souls defined.

Through trials and joys, hand in hand we go,
In the garden of life, we continue to grow.
With every heartbeat, a promise anew,
In the sanctuary's light, love shines through.

Forever shall we cherish this bond so rare,
In the sanctuary of union, suspended in air.
With open hearts and our spirits aligned,
In blissful unity, true peace we find.

The Sacred Dance of Connected Souls

In twilight's glow, our spirits arise,
Dancing beneath the vast, open skies.
With every step, a prayer we weave,
In the sacred dance, we truly believe.

Connected in rhythm, hearts held tight,
Guided by faith, we move towards the light.
A circle of love, forever we sway,
In the sacred dance, come what may.

Each twirl a blessing, each laugh a song,
In this embrace, we know we belong.
With every heartbeat, life's magic unfolds,
In the sacred dance, our story is told.

Through joy and sorrow, our spirits entwine,
In the dance of life, love's glow does shine.
With open eyes and hearts that unite,
Connected souls soar, a beautiful sight.

In the rhythm of life, we find our grace,
In the sacred dance, we hold our place.
Bound by love in this endless embrace,
Together we flourish in time and space.

The Sanctuary of Shared Breath

In the quiet of the dawn's embrace,
Whispers of serenity find their place.
Hands uplifted, hearts in prayer,
In this haven, we cast our cares.

The Sanctuary of Shared Breath

The light of kindness gently glows,
Body and spirit, they intertwine like flows.
With every breath, a promise made,
In this sanctuary, love shall not fade.

The Sanctuary of Shared Breath

Together we weave the sacred thread,
Binding our souls, where angels tread.
With faith as our guide, we journey forth,
In shared breath, we discover our worth.

The Sanctuary of Shared Breath

In the silence, hear the sacred song,
Melodies of mercy, where we all belong.
Each note a prayer, echoing bright,
In this sanctuary, we bathe in light.

The Sanctuary of Shared Breath

As shadows dance in the evening glow,
We gather strength, our spirits flow.
United we stand, with grace we tread,
In this haven, love gently spreads.

The Sanctuary of Shared Breath

So let us cherish this sacred space,
Where every heart finds its rightful place.
In the sanctuary of shared breath,
We find our lives, and conquer death.

Chords of Celestial Connection

The stars above whisper sweetly,
In hymns of love that ring so deeply.
Hearts aligned in harmony's grace,
We dance together, lost in space.

Chords of Celestial Connection

With every heartbeat, our spirits rise,
Uniting under vast, endless skies.
In the stillness, our souls can sing,
Of sacred truths that love can bring.

Chords of Celestial Connection

Tuned to the frequency of divine light,
We soar on wings, embracing the night.
This cosmic bond we shall not sever,
In chords of faith, we are forever.

Chords of Celestial Connection

Through trials faced, we find our song,
Together we grow, forever strong.
In the embrace of the universe wide,
We find our refuge, with love as our guide.

Chords of Celestial Connection

So let us cherish this celestial tune,
In the quiet hours beneath the moon.
With open hearts, together we rise,
In chords of connection that never die.

Vows Carved in Light

In sacred whispers, vows we make,
Promises of love that never break.
Under the watchful stars above,
We carve our truth in endless love.

Vows Carved in Light

With every breath, we seal our fate,
In unity, we shall not wait.
With hands entwined, we venture forth,
In sacred trust, we find our worth.

Vows Carved in Light

A tapestry woven with threads of grace,
Love finds a home in every space.
Carving our names in the fabric of night,
Eternal bonds in the soft twilight.

Vows Carved in Light

Through trials faced and storms we weather,
We stand united, hearts together.
In every tear, a lesson learned,
In every spark, our passion burned.

Vows Carved in Light

So let them witness what we have spun,
With every heartbeat, we are one.
In the echoes of love's sacred flight,
We find our souls, our vows carved in light.

The Altar of Tender Hearts

At the altar where kindness flows,
We gather strength, as love bestows.
In the softness of each gentle word,
Our spirits sing, and hearts are stirred.

The Altar of Tender Hearts

With hands held high, we pledge anew,
To nurture love in all we do.
Forgiveness blooms in sacred space,
At this altar, we find our grace.

The Altar of Tender Hearts

Each tear we shed, a healing balm,
In this embrace, we find our calm.
With loving eyes, we see the spark,
At the altar, igniting the dark.

The Altar of Tender Hearts

We honor joy, we honor pain,
In every loss, in every gain.
Together we rise, hand in hand,
At this altar, united we stand.

The Altar of Tender Hearts

So let us gather, in love's embrace,
At the altar of tender hearts, our place.
With every heartbeat, and every breath,
In love's sweet journey, we conquer death.

The Language of Sacred Feelings

In whispers soft, the heart will speak,
A sacred tongue that few can seek.
With every prayer, the soul will rise,
In gentle light, we find the skies.

Each tear a bead on Rosary's chain,
Signifying love, joy, and pain.
The vows we breathe, etched in the air,
A vow to love, a sacred prayer.

Hearts intertwined in grace divine,
In moments pure, where spirits shine.
We walk the path of holy strife,
In sacred love, we find our life.

With every heartbeat, rhythms flow,
In sacred spaces, love will grow.
With hands uplifted, we share the light,
A bond that glows, eternally bright.

Let faith be the compass showing way,
In storms we trust, in peace we stay.
For love transcends the earthly sphere,
In every breath, He's always near.

Revelations of the Inner Sanctum

In the silence deep, I find my core,
A hidden truth behind the door.
The whispers keen, my spirit wakes,
In shadows cast, the light partakes.

Every prayer a seed that's sown,
In fertile ground, the heart has grown.
Revelations clear as morning sun,
In sacred dance, we are as one.

Through trials faced, the soul ignites,
With every step, our love unites.
In stillness found, a vision clear,
Unveiling grace that draws us near.

The sacred Word, a guiding flame,
In fervent echoes, we call His name.
In laughter shared, in sorrow's veil,
We walk the path, we cannot fail.

Each moment stitched with threads of faith,
A tapestry of love, our wraith.
Embrace the truth within the heart,
In sacred realms, we'll never part.

Our spirits soar, like doves take flight,
In unity found, all hearts ignite.
Revelations bloom in every prayer,
In love's embrace, we are laid bare.

Luminous Pathways of Affection

Beneath the stars, the heart takes flight,
On luminous paths, we seek the light.
In gentle touch, affection's grace,
In every breath, we feel His face.

With hope as wings, we rise above,
Our spirits intertwined in love.
In whispered vows, our dreams collide,
On sacred journeys, we abide.

Through valleys low and mountains high,
With open hearts, we reach the sky.
Each step we take, in faith we move,
On luminous pathways, we find our groove.

In every glance, a shared delight,
A flickering flame, the heart's kite.
With every sigh, the bond grows strong,
In love's embrace, we all belong.

In unity's song, we dance and sway,
In sacred harmony, we find our way.
Luminous pathways light the night,
In every moment, His love ignites.

Celestial Strings of Yearning

In twilight's glow, our spirits yearn,
For every heart, the magic turns.
With every prayer, the strings resound,
In sacred echoes, hope is found.

Each moment felt, a pulse divine,
In whispered dreams, our souls align.
Celestial music fills the air,
In every sigh, we find our prayer.

As stars align in cosmic dance,
We trace the paths of sacred chance.
The yearnings deep within us grow,
In every heartbeat, love will show.

With open arms, we greet the day,
In all we do, His light will play.
With every glance, the strings entwine,
In harmony, our spirits shine.

Through trials faced, we stand as one,
In celestial light, our work is done.
With every chord, our voices rise,
In sacred bonds, we reach the skies.

These strings of yearning, pure and bright,
In unity found, we chase the night.
Celestial dreams in every heart,
Together, never shall we part.